WORLD OF WOW WONDER

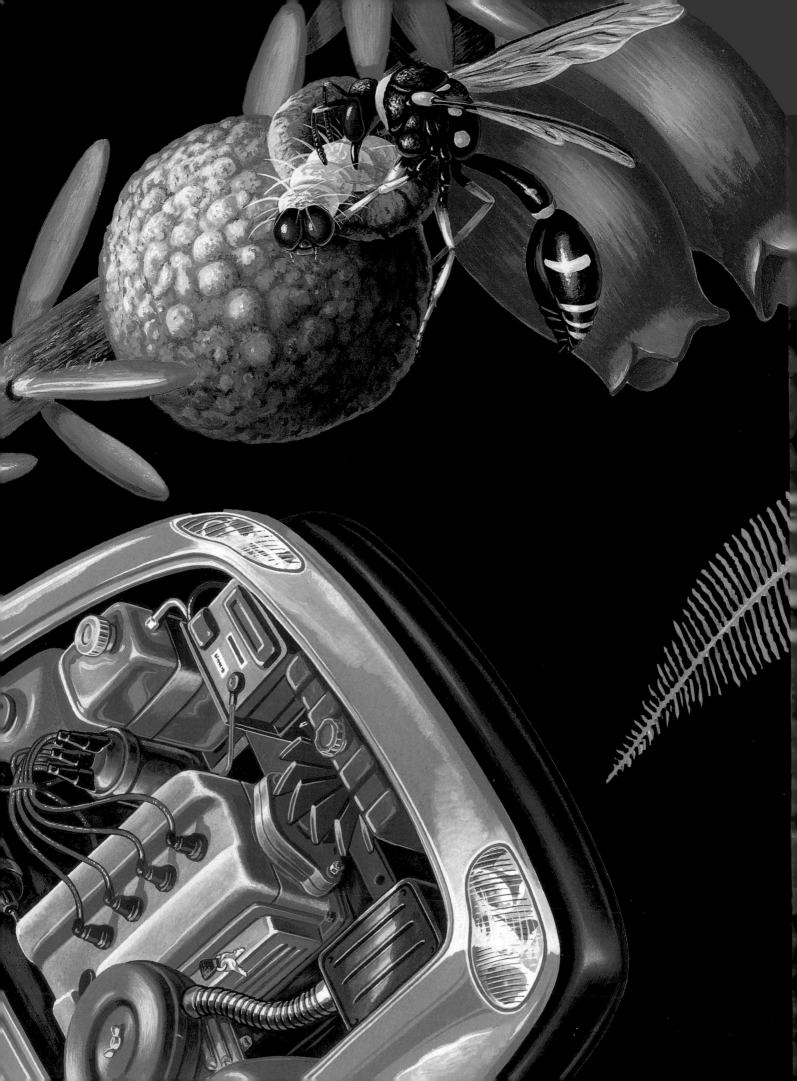

WORLD OF WOW WONDER

THE REALLY BIG

I didn't know that

Book

All about Bugs, Sharks, Dinosaurs, Cars & Trains

Get ready to hear your kids say, "Wow! I didn't know that!" as they dive into this fun, informative, question-answering series of books! Students—and teachers and parents—will learn things about the world around them that they never knew before!

This approach to education seeks to promote an interest in learning by answering questions kids have always wondered about. When books answer questions that kids already want to know the answers to, kids love to read those books, fostering a love for reading and learning, the true keys to lifelong education.

Colorful graphics are labeled and explained to connect with visual learners, while in-depth explanations of each subject will connect with those who prefer reading or listening as their learning style.

This educational series makes learning fun through many levels of interaction. The in-depth information combined with fantastic illustrations promote learning and retention, while question and answer boxes reinforce the subject matter to promote higher order thinking.

Teachers and parents love this series because it engages young people, sparking an interest and desire in learning. It doesn't feel like work to learn about a new subject with books this interactive and interesting.

This set of books will be an addition to your home or classroom library that everyone will enjoy. And, before you know it, you, too, will be saying, "Wow! I didn't know that!"

"People cannot learn by having information pressed into their brains. Knowledge has to be sucked into the brain, not pushed in. First, one must create a state of mind that craves knowledge, interest, and wonder. You can teach only by creating an urge to know." - Victor Weisskopf

I didn't know that

Concept, editorial, and design by David West Children's Books
Designer: Robert Perry
Illustrators: Myke Taylor, Rob Shone, Jo Moore
American Edition Editor:Johannah Gilman Paiva
American Redesign: Jonas Fearon Bell

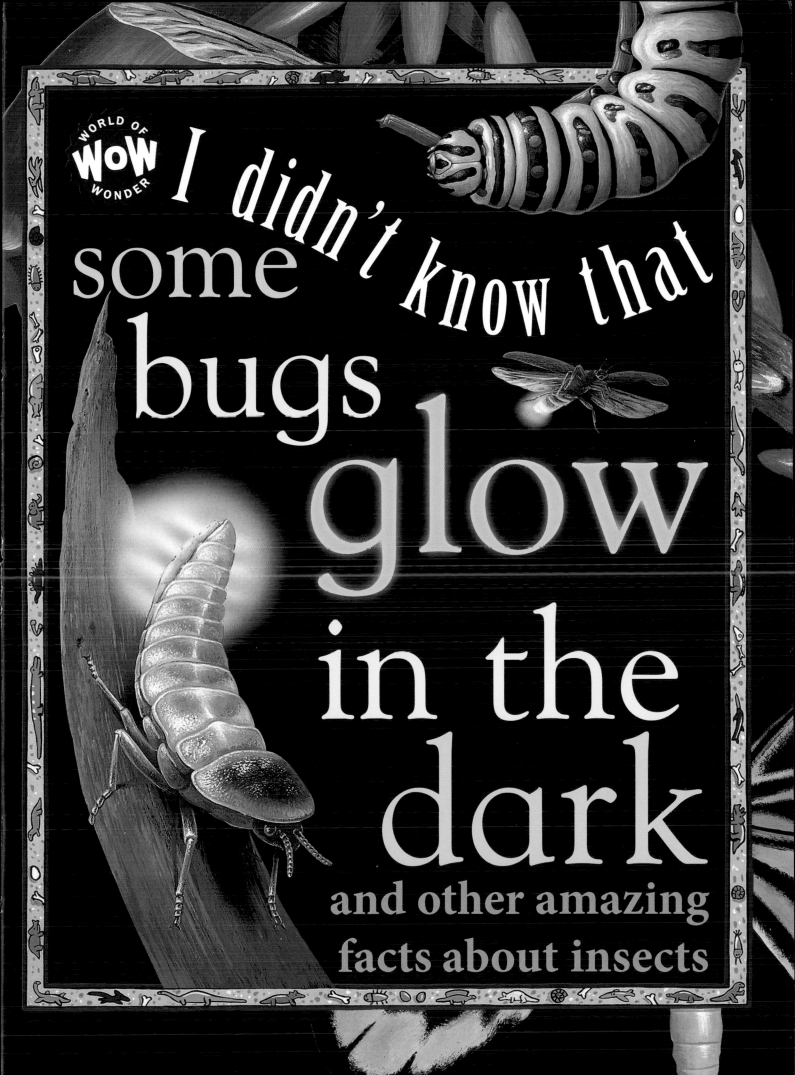

WORLD OF
WOW
WONDER

I didn't know that

some bugs glow in the dark

and other amazing facts about insects

I didn't know that

insects have six legs. Beetles, ants, and all other insects have three pairs of legs. Counting the legs is a sure way of identifying an insect. Wood lice, spiders, mites, and centipedes aren't insects— they have far too many legs.

Goliath beetle

An insect has three different parts to its body: the head, the thorax, and the abdomen. A hard outer skeleton makes the insect waterproof and protects its soft insides.

Head Eye Brain Thorax Stomach Woodlouse

Mouth Heart Leg Abdomen

The first insects lived 370 million years ago—long before the dinosaurs.

People who study insects are called "entomologists." They learn about insects, how and where they live, and how best to protect them.

Centipede

Goliath bird-eating spider

There are well over a million kinds of insects in the world. That's more than all the other kinds of animals put together! Entomologists discover 8,000 new insects every year.

I didn't know that

beetles can fly. Ladybugs and many other beetles can all fly when they need to. They open up the wingcases on their back, unfold their soft wings, and take off!

Butterfly

Dragonfly

A butterfly's wings are covered with rows of scales, arranged like the tiles on a roof. Each scale is like a tiny speck of dust.

Flying insects survive tropical storms because the raindrops make a breeze as they fall, which blows tiny insects aside. They end up flying between the drops.

! Some flies' wings can beat 1,000 times a second—that's why flies buzz.

True or False?
Flies have only one pair of wings.

Answer: **True**
Flies that have one pair of wings, such as the housefly, are called "true flies." Dragonflies and mayflies have two pairs of wings, so they're not true flies at all. Beetles have one pair of wings, but their wingcases count as a second pair— so beetles are not true flies either!

Beetle

Wasp

A wasp's second pair of wings is hard to see.

Bluebottle

Can you find five true flies?

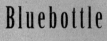

11

I didn't know that

caterpillars are baby butterflies. Like many insects, butterflies change completely as they grow from an egg, to a caterpillar, to a pupa, to a butterfly. This way of growing is called "metamorphosis."

The author Franz Kafka wrote a book called *Metamorphosis*. It's about a man who changed into a giant insect.

Can you find nine caterpillars?

Some caterpillars change into moths, not butterflies.

Not all insects change as they grow. Baby shield bugs look like their parents when they hatch. They just get bigger and bigger, and eventually grow their wings.

Mayflies spend most of their lives as wingless larvae. Once they change into adult mayflies, they only live for a day.

I didn't know that

some bugs can walk on water. Pond skaters are so light that they can skim across ponds without falling into the water. Hairy tufts on their tiny feet help them to stay afloat.

Dragonfly nymph

Pond skater

Dragonflies begin life in water as creatures called "nymphs." They will attack small fish and tadpoles that are bigger than themselves.

Tadpole

Can you find the water snail?

True or False?
Water beetles in
lakes and ponds
can breathe under the water.

Answer: **False**
Water beetles can't breathe
underwater. They swim to the
surface to collect air bubbles.
These supply the beetles
with air when they dive
underwater.

Water beetle

The ancient Greeks
and Romans believed
that beautiful nature
goddesses lived in rivers
and streams. They were
called "water nymphs."

I didn't know that

termite mounds have air-conditioning. Termites build themselves tall mud towers, where millions of the insects live. Every tower has a chimney that draws up warm air and keeps the nest cool.

Tropical weaver ants build their homes out of leaves. Some of the ants hold the leaves together, while others stick them with a sticky glue. The glue comes from larvae the ants carry in their jaws.

1

Termites make a natural cement by mixing sand with their droppings.

True or False?

Some insects live in tents in the trees.

Answer: **True**
Some caterpillars spin a huge silk canopy around their branch and stay safe and sound inside.

Insects that live together are called "social insects." Ants, termites, bees, and wasps are all social insects and live in large groups called "colonies." This is the best way for them to survive.

1. Chimney
2. Food store
3. Queen's chamber
4. Larvae galleries

17

Potter wasp

In ancient Egypt, the dung beetle was the symbol for the sun god, who rolled the sun across the sky each day.

I didn't know that

some wasps build pots. The female potter wasp makes tiny mud pots, and lays an egg in each one. Before sealing a pot, she pokes a grub inside—a tasty meal for her young when it hatches.

Dung beetle brooch from Ancient Egypt

! Most insects don't make nests. They just lay their eggs near some food.

True or False?

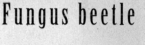 **Insects make bad parents. They never look after their young.**

Answer: **False**
The female fungus beetle cleans and protects her eggs until they hatch. Then, she helps the larvae to feed for about two weeks.

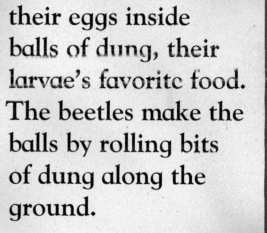

Fungus beetle

Dung beetles lay their eggs inside balls of dung, their larvae's favorite food. The beetles make the balls by rolling bits of dung along the ground.

 You can make a giant potter wasp's pot. Roll damp clay into thin ropes, and coil them in circles to make a jar. Copy the shape from the picture (above left). Be sure to make a lip around the top. Smooth the sides and leave it to dry.

! Cuckoo bees lay their eggs in other bees' nests.

I didn't know that

ants are great farmers. Just as farmers keep cows, so some kinds of ants keep aphids. The ants protect the aphids from their enemies, and in return the ants take honeydew that the aphids secrete.

 If you want to study moths, you can attract them by leaving a mixture of sugar and water near a lighted, open window at night.

Can you find the bumblebee?

Cockroaches eat anything: meat, brea[d]

Proboscis

True or False?
A honeybee tastes its food with its feet.

Answer: **True**
A honeybee tastes with its feet as well as its mouth. It can sample its food as soon as it lands on it. (So can houseflies.)

Butterflies suck up the nectar from flowers through a long tongue called a "proboscis." When they're not feeding, they keep it curled up out of the way.

ruit, cardboard...

I didn't know that

some insects eat lizards. When a praying mantis snaps its spiny legs, its helpless prey is trapped inside. Mantises are fierce hunters. Most of them eat other insects, but some catch lizards and frogs.

Praying mantis

! A female mantis is so dangerous, she'll even eat her mate.

Some tropical moths feed on the salty tears of horses and deer. The moths flutter around the animal's eyes to make them cry!

Can you find the praying mantis' meal?

Not all mosquitoes suck blood—only the females do. They need blood to make their eggs. Male mosquitoes feed on nectar.

Mosquito

When the assassin bug catches a tasty meal, it injects it with poison. This turns the prey's body to soup. Then, the bug sucks it all up.

Assassin bug

23

I didn't know that

some leaves are insects. Leaf insects look just like the leaves they feed on. They blend in so well against the background that their enemies often don't see them. This is called "camouflage."

Many animals eat caterpillars, but the hawk mouth caterpillar has a clever disguise to frighten its enemies away. It looks just like a hungry snake!

Leaf insect

Stick bug

Hawk mouth caterpillar

24

These fly orchids aren't insects at all, but plants that mimic insects. This attracts the male insect to them, that can pollinate (fertilize) them.

Camouflage isn't only for defense. The pink flower mantis is cleverly hidden inside an orchid—the better to ambush its prey.

Flower mantis

Thorn bugs

When thorn bugs land on twigs, they look like nasty thorns. And, even if they're caught, they're much too sharp to eat.

! Many insects are green so they match the leaves they feed on.

I didn't know that

some insects stink. Stinkbugs are the skunks of the insect world. When they're frightened, they let out a dreadful smell from tiny holes between their legs. This gets rid of enemies—fast!

Gypsy moth caterpillars

Gypsy moth caterpillars escape danger by dropping down on a line of silk and wafting away in the wind.

Stinkbugs

Can you find five small stinkbugs?

The weta is a huge insect, with long legs covered in spikes. When it's caught by a bird, the weta kicks with all its might, and is usually dropped in surprise!

Weta

A bombardier beetle fires at its enemies with a boiling hot stream of chemicals. It really stings!

Bombardier beetle

The screech beetle surprises its enemies with a loud squeak!

I didn't know that

some bugs glow in the dark. To find a mate, female fireflies make a light in their abdomen and flash signals to males. They are called "glowworms" or "lightning bugs."

A red mite is not an insect. It has eight legs.

Can you find the imposter?

An insect's feelers aren't just for feeling. They help it to pick up smells in the air—and tastes and sounds, too!

True or False? You could read by the light of a glowworm.

Answer: **True**
Glowworms were once used as reading lamps. Their glow lasts two hours, or more.

When an ant finds food, it marks the path to it with a strong-smelling scent. Other ants soon follow the scent and turn up to share the feast.

When two ants meet, they often touch feelers in greeting.

I didn't know that

a stick bug is the biggest insect in the world. The Indonesian giant stick bug measures more than 12 inches (30 centimeters) from head to toe. It's so big that it moves very slowly.

Male cicadas are the loudest insects in the world. Their clicking noise can be heard by female cicadas half a mile away.

Can you find 10 fairy flies?

It's difficult to see real fairy flies—they are the size of a pin.

Five hundred years ago, rat fleas were the most dangerous insects in the world. They spread a deadly sickness called "the plague," which killed millions and millions of people.

When the Queen Alexandra birdwing butterfly spreads its wings, it measures 11 inches (28 centimeters) from wing tip to wing tip. No wonder it's mistaken for a bird!

! Fleas can jump an incredible 130 times their own height.

Glossary

Abdomen
The last of the three parts of an insect's body.

Aphids
Tiny insects, such as greenflies, that feed by sucking up the juices from plants.

Beetles
A group of insects that has hard wingcases and can usually fly.

Camouflage
The colors and markings on an insect that help it to blend in with its surroundings, and make it difficult to see them.

Caterpillar
The larva of a moth or butterfly.

Crickets
A group of insects that are related to grasshoppers and make a loud chirping noise.

Grub
The young caterpillar-like stage of a beetle and some other insects.

Larva (plural: Larvae)
The young stage of an insect before metamorphosis.

Caterpillars, maggots, and grubs are all larvae.

Metamorphosis
The change from the young stage to the adult stage of an insect. Many insects change from a larva, to a pupa, to a fully-grown adult.

Nectar
The sweet liquid inside flowers, which attracts insects and other animals.

Nymph
The young stage of an insect that hatches looking just like its parents.

Pupa
The stage in an insect's life when it develops inside a hard, protective case.

Queen
The only egg-laying female in a nest of social insects,

such as termites and bees.

Thorax
The middle part of an insect's body, between the head and abdomen.

Wingcases
Hard outer wings that are not used for flying.

34

WORLD OF WOW WONDER

35

I didn't know that

Concept, editorial, and design by David West Children's Books
Designer: Robert Perry
Illustrators: Darren Harvey-Wildlife Art Ltd, Jo Moore
American Edition Editor:Johannah Gilman Paiva
American Redesign: Jonas Fearon Bell

WORLD OF **WOW** WONDER

I didn't know that

sharks keep losing their teeth

I didn't know that

sharks are older than dinosaurs. Sharks' ancestors lived about 200 million years before dinosaurs. Some were giants and had spines on their head.

Can you find five trilobites?

Just a few sharks turned into fossils, but many of their teeth did! This tooth (left) measures almost 5 inches (12 centimeters) long, and belonged to a monster shark called "megalodon." A great white shark's tooth is half this size.

Cladoselache lived about 350 million years ago, and measured about 6.5 feet (2 meters) from teeth to tail. The shark's mouth was at the tip of its snout, not tucked underneath like most sharks today.

Cladoselache

This fossil of a shark called "stethacanthus" shows that it had thorny spines. Fossils of sharks are rare because their skeletons are made not of bone, but cartilage, which rots away before it can fossilize.

! Port Jackson sharks still have spines, just like their ancestors did.

I didn't know that

sharks are the biggest fish.
The whale shark measures up to
42 feet (13 meters) long, and is
the largest fish in the sea. This
gentle giant feeds peacefully,
filtering tiny plants and animals
from the water.

Can you find three divers?

Whale shark

The dwarf shark
is just 6 inches
(15 centimeters)
long, not much
bigger than a
goldfish. In
fact, half of all
known sharks
measure less
than 3 feet
(1 meter) long.

Whale sharks are so gentle that divers can ride on them.

To see how big a whale shark really is, try making one in the park or on the beach. Using a yardstick (or meterstick) as a guide, measure out its length, then fill in the outline with pebbles or twigs.

The basking shark is the world's second largest fish. It swims with its mouth open to catch microscopic sea creatures.

Megamouth shark

I didn't know that

some sharks glow in the dark. Some sharks that live in the deep, dark parts of the ocean make their own light. The jaws of a megamouth shark give out a silvery glow. This probably helps attract tasty shrimp.

Can you find six jellyfish?

The frilled shark had elongated eyes to see in the murky depths.

The goblin shark (above) lives at the bottom of the sea. Its long, sensitive snout helps it find any nearby prey.

Sensitive snout

Lantern sharks (left) glow in the water, thanks to a shiny slime on their skin. Experts think the coloring may help sharks attract their prey or keep their place in a shoal.

The cookie-cutter shark gets its name from its curious bite. When the shark attacks another animal, it leaves a wound that is perfectly round—just like a cookie.

I didn't know that

some sharks have heads like hammers. The hammerhead shark has a "T" shaped head, just like the top of a hammer. As the shark swims, it swings its head from side to side so its eyes have an all-around view.

Great hammerhead shark

The wobbegong is a strange looking shark with speckled skin and tassels that make it look like a rock or seaweed. The fish makes use of this brilliant camouflage by hiding on the seabed and snapping up fish.

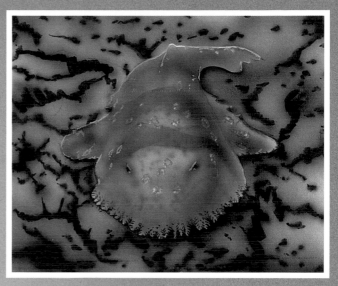

Stingray

Gill slits

Sharks are related to rays (left). Both groups of fish have gill slits instead of flaps, and skeletons of cartilage rather than bone.

 True or False?
Some sharks have wings.

Answer: **True**
The angel shark's large fins (right) are just like wings. It uses them to glide along the seabed as it searches for crustaceans and fish.

Angel sharks are called "monkfish" since they seem to be wearing a hood.

I didn't know that

if sharks stop swimming, they sink. Most fish have an air-filled bladder inside them, which helps keep them afloat in the sea. Sharks don't have swim bladders. To avoid sinking, most sharks have to swim all the time, like they are treading water.

 True or False?
Sharks sleep in caves.

Answer: **True**
The white-tip reef shark is a sleepy fish. At night, it cruises sluggishly around coral reefs, and spends the day sleeping on the seabed. It often hides away in caves to avoid being spotted and disturbed.

! The pectoral fins give a shark lift, just like the wings on a plane.

A shark's body is sleek, streamlined, and built for speed. Its fins are large and fairly stiff, and help it power forward, stay upright, steer, and stop.

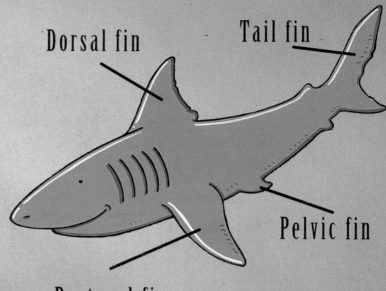

Dorsal fin

Tail fin

Pelvic fin

Pectoral fin

Mako shark

Like all fish, sharks have gills to take in oxygen from water. As water flows over the gills, tiny blood vessels absorb the oxygen and carry it around the body.

47

I didn't know that

sharks keep losing their teeth.
Sharks often lose their teeth as
they attack their prey, so new
teeth constantly grow inside their
mouths. Slowly, the new teeth form
and move outwards to replace the
older ones.

Can you find five teeth?

Sand tiger shark

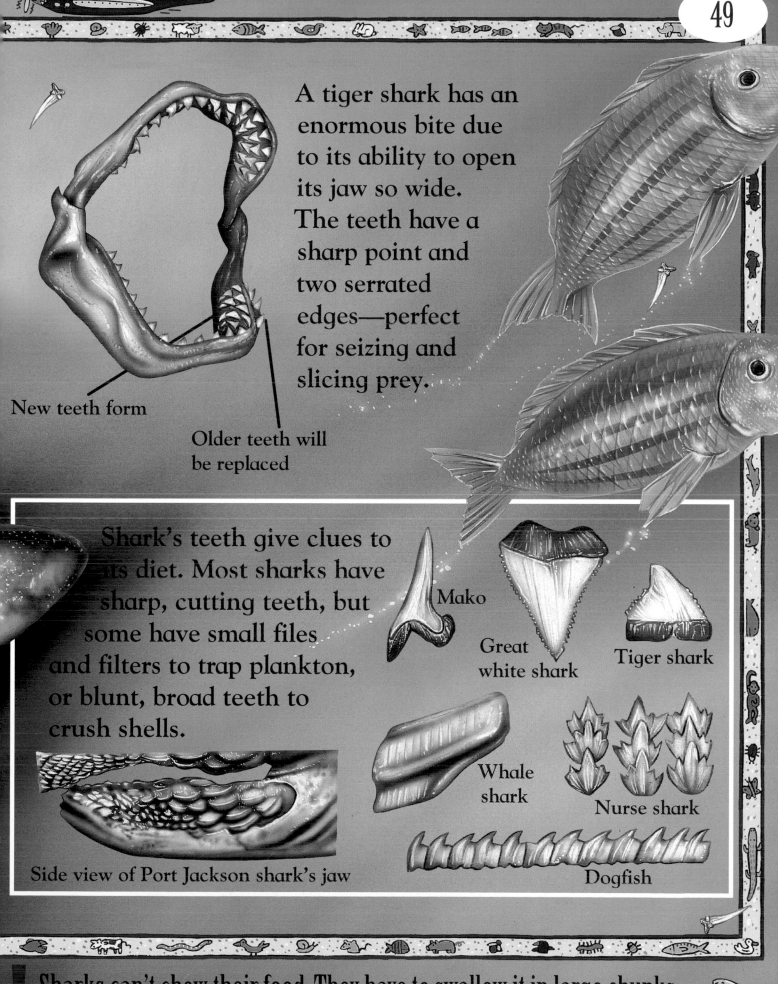

A tiger shark has an enormous bite due to its ability to open its jaw so wide. The teeth have a sharp point and two serrated edges—perfect for seizing and slicing prey.

New teeth form

Older teeth will be replaced

Shark's teeth give clues to its diet. Most sharks have sharp, cutting teeth, but some have small files and filters to trap plankton, or blunt, broad teeth to crush shells.

Mako

Great white shark

Tiger shark

Whale shark

Nurse shark

Side view of Port Jackson shark's jaw

Dogfish

Sharks can't chew their food. They have to swallow it in large chunks.

I didn't know that

sharks feed in a frenzy. When sharks feed, others may join in. As they snap at the food, they get excited by the blood and movement in the water. They can bite or kill each other during this "feeding frenzy."

A shark's jaw lies a long way under its pointed snout. As the fish lunges to bite, it lifts its nose out of the way, and swings its jaws forward. Then, it rolls up its eyes inside its head to protect them during the attack.

Sharks eat all kinds of foods: seabirds, seals, turtles, crustaceans, and plankton. They rarely eat people; they don't like the taste of human flesh!

Blue sharks

 True or False?
Some sharks attack with their tail.

Answer: **True**
The thresher shark has a long tail, which it lashes in the water like a whip. Scientists think that this either stuns its prey or herds fish into a tightly-knit group, which the thresher shark then attacks.

❗ ...an old tire, three raincoats, an anchor, and an oil drum.

I didn't know that

sharks can smell blood over a half mile (1 kilometer) away. Sharks have a keen sense of smell. As water streams past their nostrils, they pick up messages in the sea around them. When sharks sniff the blood of a wounded animal, they can power toward it.

Sharks have tiny organs on their snout that can pick up electrical signals. Since every creature in the sea produces some kind of electricity, these organs help sharks to hunt them down.

Shark skin was once used on sword handles to give a good grip.

Sharks have a lateral line on each side of their body, which picks up vibrations in the sea. It helps sharks to feel the things that are moving around them, such as a seal or a fish.

Can you find the other fish?

Oceanic white-tip shark

A shark's body is covered not with scales, but with tooth-like bumps called "denticles." These are very coarse, and feel rough if they're stroked the wrong way.

53

I didn't know that

some fish hitch rides on sharks. Remoras are small fish with a sucker pad on their head. They use it to cling onto sharks. As they ride, they help by eating parasites on the sharks.

Sucker pad

Can you find ten remoras?

Remoras ride on the waves made by sharks, just like they are surfing.

Zebra shark

Small, agile pilot fish often swim alongside a shark. They probably feel safe near their large companion, and can also feed on scraps of its food.

I didn't know that

some baby sharks grow inside leather purses. Some sharks lay their eggs in leathery cases called "mermaid purses." Inside the purse, the eggs grow into baby sharks. They eat the yolk and hatch 10 months later.

Can you find the mother shark?

Swell shark embryos

Seven months old

56

While some kinds of sharks hatch out of eggs, most develop inside their mother's body. They feed either on egg yolk or on food in their mother's blood, and are later born live, like mammals.

A baby lemon shark emerges from its mother.

Next time you're on the beach, try to find a mermaid's purse. The dogfish is a common shark, and its dry, black egg cases are often washed up on the shore.

Many sharks try to protect their eggs. The horn shark wedges her spiral-shaped egg case into a crack in a rock. Other egg cases have long tendrils that cling onto plants.

Horn shark egg

! A whale shark's egg is the size of a football.

I didn't know that

people are sharks' worst enemies. Large, meat-eating sharks have no enemies in the sea, but people kill them for sport, and for their meat, skin, and oil. Also, many sharks get trapped in fishing nets and drown.

Great white shark

True or False?
Sharks are blood-thirsty killers.

Answer: **False**
This is a myth that films, such as *Jaws* have helped to spread. Most sharks leave people alone. Scientists believe attacks only happen when a shark mistakes a swimmer for a seal or other kind of prey.

Seal

Surfer

Bull shark

Some people catch sharks for sport, and treat their bodies as trophies. Every year, the number of large sharks in the sea falls.

Sharks are killed so people can make soup from their fins, jewelry from their teeth, and medicines and lipsticks from their oil.

Shark liver oil pills

Shark fin soup

Jewelry

Cosmetics

Sharks seem to attack more men than women.

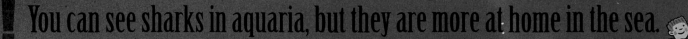

I didn't know that

shark scientists wear chain mail. Divers who study sharks need protection. Many wear chain mail suits called "neptunics," which are made from thousands of stainless steel rings. Sharks can't bite through the heavy suits.

Blue shark

To study sharks, scientists need to be able to follow them. They do this by catching sharks, attaching sonic tags to their fins, and then returning them to the water. The tags give out radio signals, which the scientists carefully track.

Sonic tag

Tiger shark

Tagging pole

Underwater photographers can safely film sharks from inside strong metal cages. It can still be a scary ordeal, though. Scientists attract the sharks with a strong-smelling bait. Sometimes the sharks crash heavily against the cage, trying to get inside!

Great white shark

The bubbles from a diver's aqualung scare some sharks.

Glossary

Bait
Food, such as a dead fish, which is used to attract sharks.

Camouflage
The colors and markings on an animal that help it to blend in with its surroundings.

Cartilage
The material that forms the skeletons of sharks and rays.

Crustacean
An animal, such as a lobster or a crab, that has a hard outer shell and lots of legs.

Fossil
Animal remains, which have turned to stone over millions of years.

Hibernate
To spend the winter in a kind of deep sleep.

Mammal
An animal, such as a cat, that gives birth to its young and feeds it on milk.

Organ
Any part of the body that has a special purpose, such as the eyes, which are the organs of sight, and the ears, which are the organs of hearing.

Parasite
An animal that lives on another animal (known as the host) and gets food from it. A parasite always damages its host.

Plankton
Microscopic plants and animals that live in the sea.

Ray
A kind of large, flat sea fish with wing-like fins and a long tail.

Serrated
Having a sharp, zig-zagging edge like a saw.

Streamlined
Having a smooth body shape that moves easily through the water.

Tapeworm
A long, flat worm that lives inside the stomach and intestines of other animals. It is a parasite.

Vibration
A shaking movement that is often felt rather than seen.

Yolk
The yellow part inside an egg, which provides food for the growing animal.

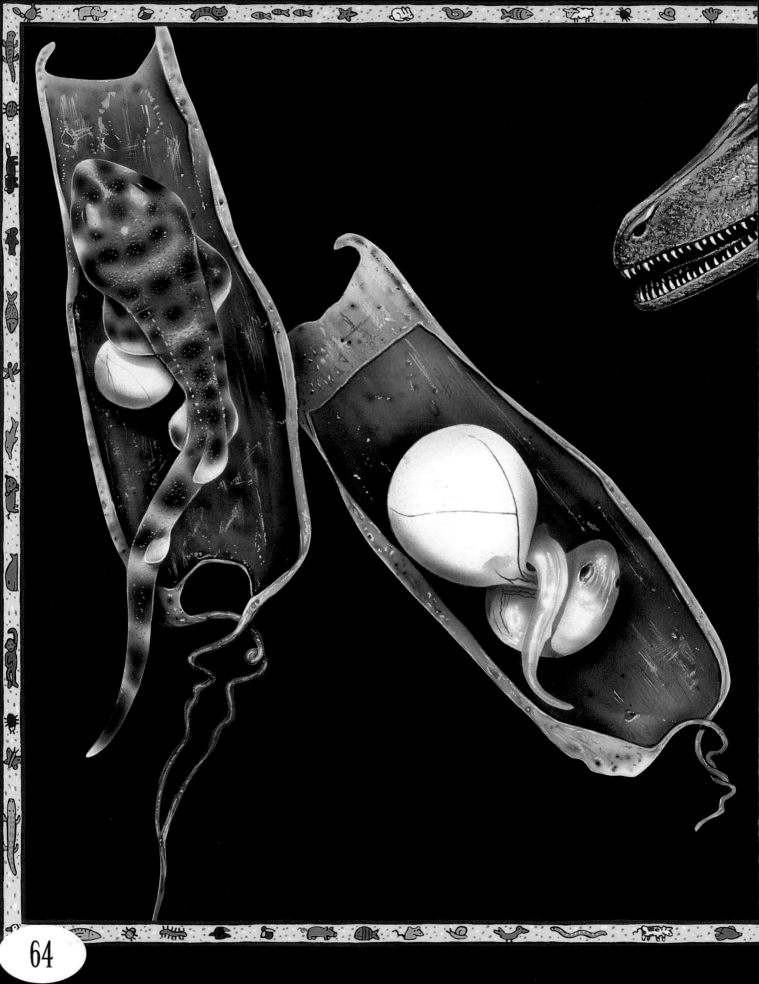

I didn't know that

Concept, editorial, and design by David West Children's Books
Designer: Robert Perry
Illustrators: James Field-Simon Girling and Associates, Mike Lacy, Jo Moore
American Edition Editor:Johannah Gilman Paiva
American Redesign: Jonas Fearon Bell

WORLD OF
WOW
WONDER

I didn't know that

dinosaurs

laid

eggs

I didn't know that

all dinosaurs died out 65 million years ago. For 150 million years, Earth was a planet inhabited by dinosaurs—until disaster struck. Maybe a meteorite hit the Earth, or maybe a large number of volcanoes erupted, but the dinosaurs were no more.

We know about dinosaurs because people have discovered their fossilized remains in rocks. Fossil specialists, or paleontologists, can piece fossils together and figure out how the dinosaurs lived.

True or False?
Humans were responsible for making the dinosaurs extinct.

Answer: **False**
Humans and dinosaurs never lived together on Earth. Over 60 million years separate the last dinosaurs and our earliest ancestors.

One Million Years B.C.—films that got it wrong!

Saltasaurus

Dinosaur history is divided into three periods: Triassic (early), Jurassic (middle), and Cretaceous (late). Different dinosaurs lived in different periods.

Coelophysis

Stegosaurus

Tyrannosaurus

| Triassic | Jurassic | Cretaceous |

! Crocodiles have barely changed at all since dinosaur times.

I didn't know that

dinosaur means "terrible lizard." By 1841, people realized that these enormous fossilized bones belonged to huge extinct reptiles, not giant humans! Scientist Dr. Richard Owen named them "dino" (terrible) "saurs" (lizards).

One of the differences between dinosaurs and other reptile families, such as crocodiles or lizards, is that dinosaurs walked on straight legs.

A dinosaur's skin would have been very tough and scaly to the touch. Like a snake's skin, which people sometimes expect to be slimy, it would have felt dry and bumpy.

Thirty-nine feet (almost 12 meters) tall with a three-foot (almost one meter) wide mouth, and teeth as long as carving knives, Tyrannosaurus rex was a nightmare lizard! Its name means "King Tyrant Lizard."

Close-up of T. rex's skin

T. rex's fossilized tooth

The first dinosaur discovered in the West was found in 1824.

I didn't know that

some dinosaurs were bigger than a four-story building. Ultrasaurus was a huge sauropod, the biggest dinosaur ever at 98 feet (almost 30 meters) long and 39 feet (almost 12 meters) high. A human would barely have reached its ankles!

72

Can you find nine Compsognathuses?

Fossilized footprints show that the enormous sauropods moved in groups, walking with long strides. Some might have swum across rivers, pulling themselves along with their front legs.

The chicken-sized Compsognathus was one of the smallest dinosaurs. It was a speedy meat-eater, which chased after tiny mammals, lizards, and insects.

! Mamenchisaurus had a 33 foot (10 meter) long neck!

I didn't know that

some dinosaurs hunted in packs. Fossils have been found of a group of Deinonychuses surrounding a Tenontosaurus, an herbivore. They probably hunted together, like lions or wolves.

Deinonychus

Deinonychus had long claws for stabbing and cutting. On each hind foot, it had a special slashing claw, which could be pulled back when it ran.

A hug from Deinocheirus, "terrible hand," would have been deadly! Its arms were over eight feet (2.4 meters) long. This birdlike creature was probably bigger than T. rex.

Deinocheirus

Tenontosaurus

All meat-eating dinosaurs were theropods, with three toes and long claws. Most walked on two legs.

Apatosaurus

I didn't know that

most dinosaurs ate plants. The earliest dinosaurs were meat-eaters, but by the Jurassic period, plant-eaters were flourishing. There was still no grass to graze on—instead they grazed on other plants.

Sauropods—like Diplodocus and Apatosaurus—had teeth-like pegs for raking leaves, or spoon-shaped ones for pulling leaves off a plant. They swallowed without chewing.

Big plant-eating dinosaurs had to eat 400 pounds of leaves a day!

Hadrosaurs (duckbills like Parasaurolophus and Edmontosaurus) could eat Christmas trees! They ground twigs and pine needles between jaws that contained more than a thousand teeth pressed together into ridged plates.

Scientists can also learn about dinosaur diets from their fossilized droppings, which might contain seeds, leaves, or fish scales.

Ceratopsian dinosaurs (like Centrosaurus) had parrot-like beaks for cropping very tough plants, and strong jaws and sharp teeth for cutting them up.

I didn't know that

some dinosaurs went fishing. Baryonyx, "heavy claw," was discovered in 1983. It had unusually long, curved claws and a fossilized fish in its stomach. Scientists thought the claws were used for hooking fish out of the water.

Millions of years after the crime, a fossilized Oviraptor, "egg thief," was caught! It had a telltale pair of prongs in its otherwise toothless mouth. They were probably used for cracking the eggs it stole.

True or False?
Some dinosaurs had no teeth at all.

Answer: **True**
The birdlike Gallimimus, an ornithopod, had no teeth. Twice the size of an ostrich, it fed on insects and anything it could swallow whole.

Like snakes, dinosaurs also swallowed a meal without chewing. The fossilized skeleton of a Compsognathus (see page 71) was discovered with a whole, fossilized lizard in its stomach.

I didn't know that

dinosaurs laid eggs. They did— just like all reptiles. The dinosaur mother would scrape out a hollow nest in the ground and cover the eggs to keep them warm. She would bring food to her babies until they could leave the nest.

True or False?

The biggest dinosaurs laid giant eggs more than three feet (1 meter) long.

Answer: **False**
Even the biggest dinosaur eggs were no more than five times the size of a chicken's egg. A bigger egg would need to have a thicker shell, which would suffocate the baby.

Can you find the imposter?

Fossilized footprints of small tracks surrounded by larger ones show that young dinosaurs on the move were protected by the older, larger ones.

Like a cuckoo, the Troodon may have laid its eggs in others' nests.

I didn't know that

some dinosaurs were armor-plated. This was protection from the fierce meat-eaters, such as Carnotaurus, that hunted them. Like armadillos and porcupines today, certain plant-eaters had tough skins or spikes.

Carnotaurus

Euoplocephalus

Euoplocephalus even had bony eyelids! It also had spikes and a lethal clubbed tail for defense—enough to make any predator think twice.

Sauropods were protected by sheer size, but a group of Triceratops could make a wall of horns that would scare off their enemies.

Tyrannosaurus rex

Triceratops

True or False?
The spiny plates on a Stegosaurus (right) were for protection.

Answer: **False**
They were probably for controlling its body heat. Blood so near the skin's surface could warm up very quickly in the sun, or cool down in the shade.

! Diplodocus used its tail as a defensive whip.

I didn't know that

some dinosaurs had head-butting contests. Like rams and stags today, "boneheads," such as Stegoceras, battled for leadership. Their skulls were 10 inches (25 centimeters) thick, so it probably didn't hurt very much.

Some duck-billed dinosaurs, like
Parasaurolophus, had hollow headpieces
that were connected to their nasal passages.
They might have snored! They didn't use
their crests for fighting head-to-head.

Can
you find
the chameleon?

No one knows what colors dinosaurs
were. Like reptiles and birds today,
they were probably colored to
blend in with their surroundings.
Like chameleons, some might
have changed color.

I didn't know that

Dimorphodon

Rhamphorhynchus

Quetzalcoatlus was bigger than a hang glider. With a wingspan of 32 feet (almost 10 meters), it was the biggest creature ever to take to the air, gliding on warm air currents. Flying reptiles were not dinosaurs, but pterosaurs.

True or False?
Pterosaurs had feathers.

Answer: False
More like bats than birds, pterosaurs like Dimorphodon had furry bodies and leathery wings. They had beaked faces, but they also had teeth.

Pteranodon

The winged dinosaur, Archaeopteryx, was probably the first bird.

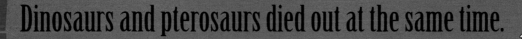

Quetzalcoatlus

Pteranodon swooped down from the cliff tops to catch fish from the sea. The crest on its head helped it to steer.

Pterodaustro also ate fish. It had a sieve in its beak so it could strain tiny fish as it flew low over the water.

I didn't know that

there were real sea monsters in dinosaur times. Dinosaurs didn't live in the sea, but it was full of all sorts of other huge and strange-looking swimming reptiles. They fed on fish and shellfish.

Elasmosaurus

The plesiosaur Elasmosaurus was 50 feet (15 meters) long, and nearly all neck. Swimming through the water, it must have looked like Diplodocus with flippers!

! The turtle-like Archelon was longer than a rowboat.

Ichthyosaurs were some of the earliest sea reptiles. They looked like dolphins and, like dolphins, breathed air. They fed on the ammonites and belemnites often found as fossils today.

Ichthyosaurs

Liopleurodon was one of the short-necked plesiosaurs. It really was a monster—its head was seven feet (over two meters) long!

Mosasaurus

Liopleurodon

Mosasaurs were some of the last sea reptiles and, at 33 feet (10 meters) long, the largest lizards ever. They looked like dragons, but with flippers rather than legs.

I didn't know that

some dinosaurs had feathers. A fossil of a feathered dinosaur was found in China in 1996. New discoveries can change the way we think about dinosaurs. Just imagine how different they would look with feathers!

 Paleontologists piece together dinosaur bones into skeletons, then flesh out the skeletons. They have to guess the colors. Take your own dinosaur models and paint them. What colors will you choose and why?

Close-up view of feathers

Mosasaurs were some of the last sea reptiles and, at 33 feet (10 meters) long, the largest lizards ever. They looked like dragons, but with flippers rather than legs.

Even though the feathers were probably for warmth rather than for flying, this find makes it even more likely that modern birds are related to dinosaurs.

Glossary

Ammonites
Prehistoric shellfish, commonly found as fossils.

Belemnites
Prehistoric bull-shaped shellfish, also common fossils.

Boneheads
The nickname given to Pachycephalosaurus. They were two-legged dinosaurs with incredibly thick skulls.

Ceratopsians
Dinosaurs that had horns and a protective bony frill.

Fossils
The remains of living things that have been preserved in rock.

Hadrosaurs
Duck-billed dinosaurs, often with a crest on their head.

Herbivore
Any plant-eater.

Ichthyosaurs
Dolphin-like sea reptiles that lived at the same time as dinosaurs.

Mosasaurs
Dragon-like sea reptiles that lived at the same time as dinosaurs.

Ornithopods
A group of dinosaurs that walked on two legs. Most were herbivores.

Paleontologists
Scientists who study the fossilized remains of extinct animals and plants.

Plesiosaurs
Sea reptiles, with flippers rather than legs, that lived at the same time as dinosaurs.

Pterosarus
A group of flying reptiles that lived at the same time as dinosaurs.

Sauropods
A group of long-necked, long-tailed, four-legged, plant-eating dinosaurs. They included Diplodocus and Apatosaurus.

Theropods
A group of meat-eating dinosaurs. Most of them walked on two legs. They included Deinonychus.

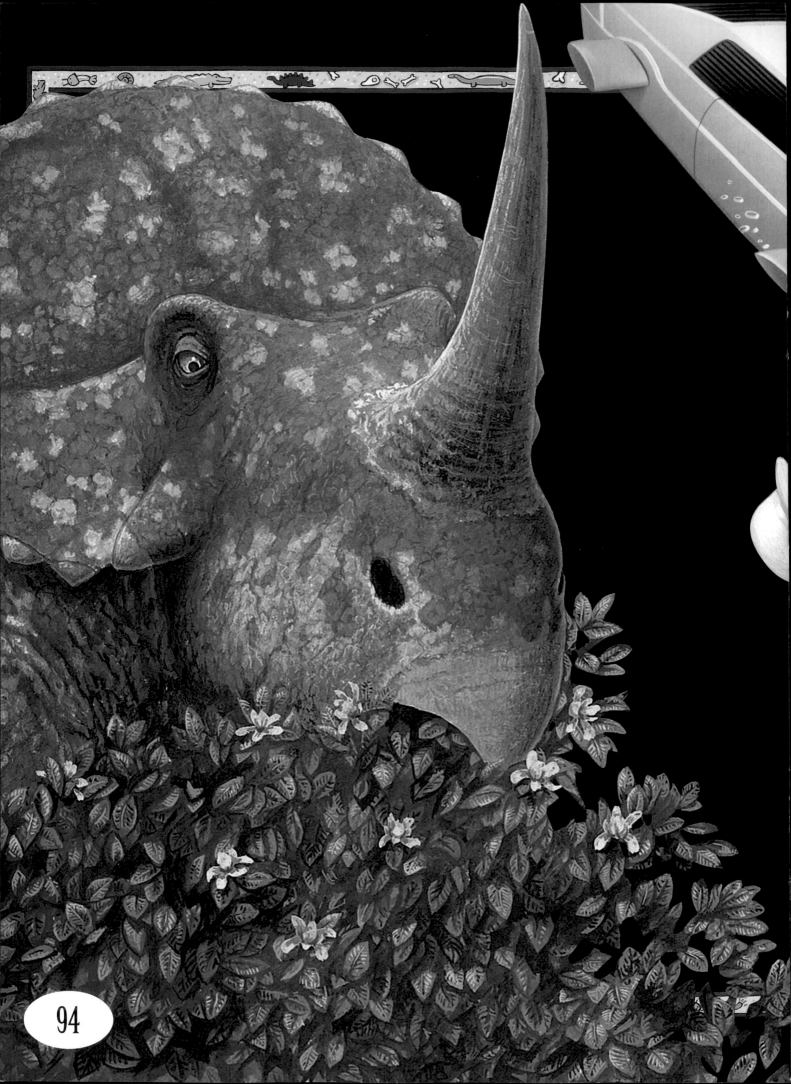

I didn't know that

Concept, editorial, and design by David West Children's Books
Designer: Simon Morse
Illustrators: Gerald Whitcomb and Don Simpson-Spec Arts, Jo Moore
American Edition Editor:Johannah Gilman Paiva
American Redesign: Jonas Fearon Bell

I didn't know that

the first cars had three wheels. The first successful car was the Benz Motorwagen. It had three wheels, a gasoline engine, and a top speed of 20 miles (30 kilometers) per hour.

Karl Benz

Gottlieb Daimler

The Bordino Steam Carriage of 1854 replaced horses with steam power. It was very heavy and cumbersome, and slower than traveling by train. The gasoline engine made such "horseless carriages" look old-fashioned.

Karl Benz and Gottlieb Daimler built the Motorwagen in Mannheim, Germany, in 1886. Do you recognize their names?

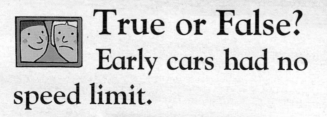

True or False?
Early cars had no speed limit.

Answer: **False.** The 1865 British law said that cars must follow a man with a red flag at less than 4 miles (6.5 kilometers) per hour.

! Since early cars were open, coats and hats were essential!

I didn't know that

cars are powered by explosions. Gasoline explodes inside a car's engine. The force created by the explosion pushes the pistons, which turn the wheels of the car.

Can you find the car keys?

An internal combustion engine works in four stages, which make up one cycle:
1. Gasoline and air mixture are sucked into cylinder.
2. Mixture is compressed.
3. Spark causes explosion.
4. Waste gases are expelled.

True or False?
All cars have engines under the hood.

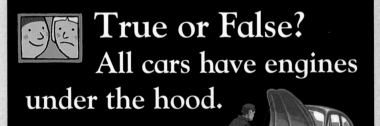

Answer: False. Some, such as the Volkswagen Beetle and the Fiat Seicento, have the engine in the trunk! Under the hood, there is space for luggage.

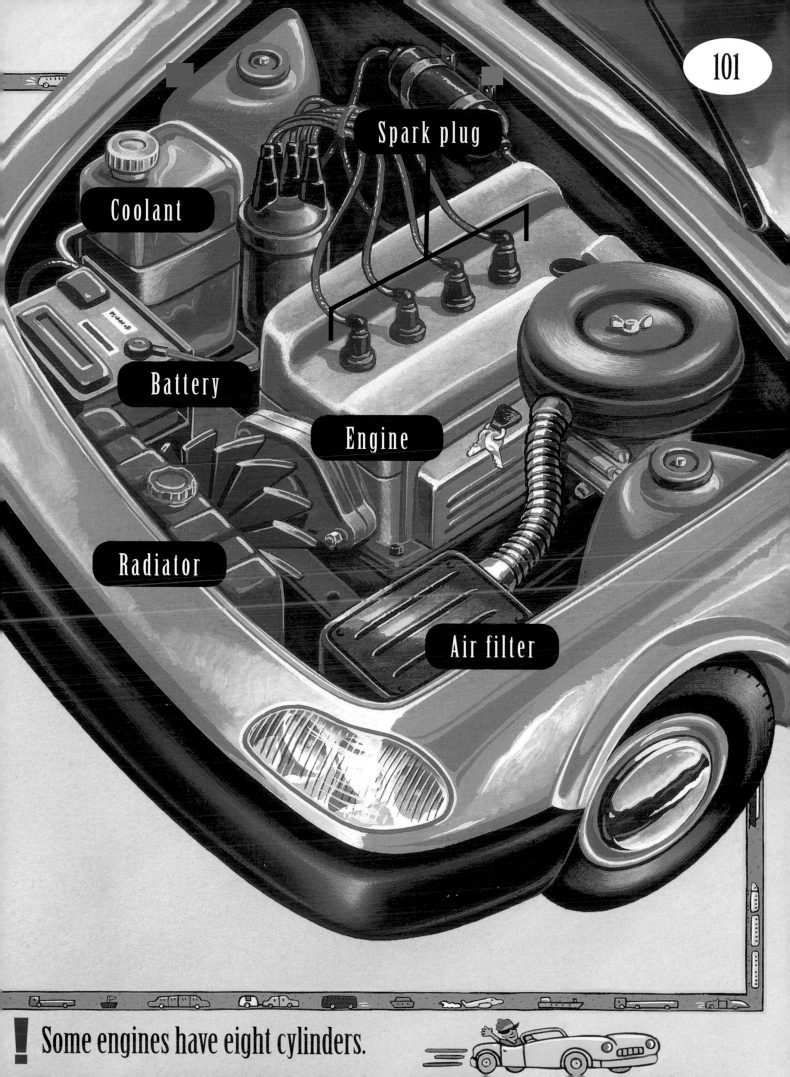

Coolant

Spark plug

Battery

Engine

Radiator

Air filter

! Some engines have eight cylinders.

I didn't know that

robots build cars. Modern cars are built quickly and accurately by robots, each with its own task. Robots can work in conditions that are too hot, noisy, or dangerous for humans.

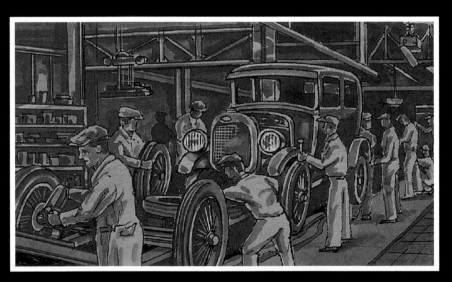

The Model-T Ford was the world's first ever mass-produced car. In 1914, Henry Ford invented the production line for building cars.

Today, modern cars are designed using computers. Designers can easily see what the finished car will look like. Then, a life-sized clay model of the car is tested in a wind tunnel for aerodynamic properties.

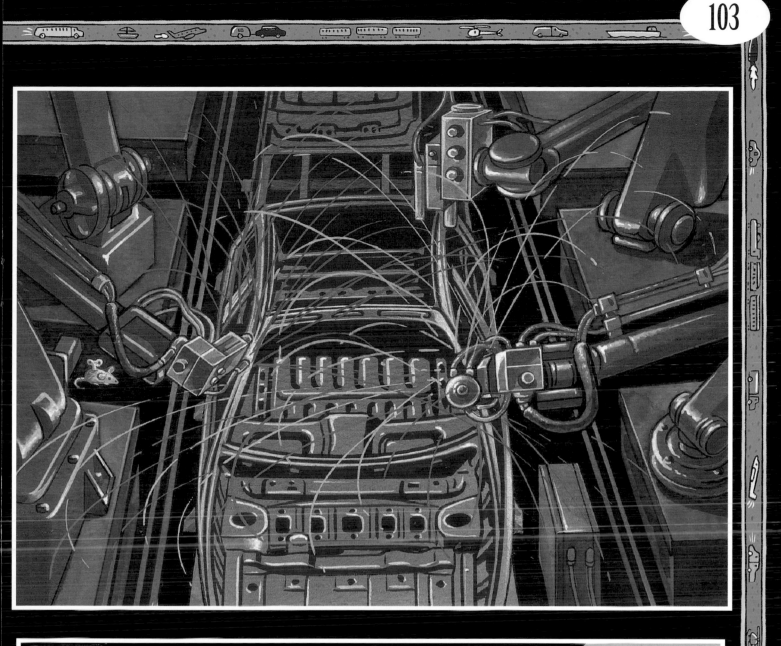

Air travels more easily over smooth surfaces than blunt ones. Cover one car with an L-shaped strip of cardstock and the other with a smooth, curved strip. Roll both cars down a slope, blowing a hair drier set on cold at them. Which one wins and why?

All the cars in the world, end-to-end, would go around the world 34 times.

I didn't know that

the best car in the world is a ghost. The Rolls Royce Silver Ghost is renowned for its superb engine and stylish looks. Some people consider it to be the best car in the world.

The stylish 1935 Auburn Speedster was perfect for cruising around glamorous Hollywood. Each car came with a plaque certifying that it had been driven at over 99 miles (160 kilometers) per hour by racing driver Ab Jenkins.

The most expensive car ever was the enormous Bugatti Royale. It was 22 feet (6.7 meters) long! Only six of them were ever made. In 1990, a Royale was sold at an auction for $15 million.

One of the greatest Grand Prix cars of all time was the 1937 Mercedes W125. With the help of two enormous superchargers, it reached speeds of almost 199 miles (320 kilometers) per hour!

I didn't know that

a T-bird is a car. In the 1950s, Ford offered a $250 suit to whoever named their sporty new car. Thunderbird (an Australian bird), or "T-bird" for short, was the winner.

Can you find the three cola bottles?

As later Thunderbirds got bigger, the Ford Company built the Mustang—a smaller sports car, very popular with young Americans. Over a million were sold in three years.

The Volkswagen Beetle is the best-selling car ever. Over 20 million have been sold! They were designed and built in Germany in the 1930s to boost the German economy and provide a cheap, reliable "people's car."

The Mini was designed in the 1950s as a cheap and efficient car for city driving. Minis are incredibly compact, and the Mini is the model for most small cars today. In a famous scene from the film *The Italian Job*, one was used to escape from a bank robbery.

❗ In 2000, 25 Austrians got in one Volkswagen Beetle!

I didn't know that

dummies test cars. Before they go on the market, new cars are tested for safety with crash test dummies—accurate models of human beings—in crash situations.

Can you find the crash test bear?

In order to see how safe a new car will be in the event of an accident, different kinds of crashes are simulated. Cars have to be able to protect passengers from front and side impacts.

Gas chemicals

Igniter

Chemicals will inflate an airbag in 40 milliseconds—that is less than a third of the time it takes to blink!

True or False?
Some cars are armor-plated.

Answer: **True.**
This Zil limousine, used by Russian presidents, could be the safest car in the world! It weighs six tons and is covered with almost three-inch- (75 millimeter-) thick steel armor plating.

! Early brakes often failed.

I didn't know that

some cars have wings. Formula One cars, which go up to 208 miles (336 kilometers) per hour, are designed with upside-down wings, which push the car downward. This makes them handle better.

Formula One cars need to have different types of tires for wet, dry, and snowy weather. Sometimes the tires are changed mid-race.

Slick tire

Wet weather tire

110

Every year, drivers compete in up to 16 Grand Prix races around the world. Each race is at least 186 miles (300 kilometers) long. The most difficult race in is Monaco, where drivers have to negotiate narrow city streets at high speeds.

True or False?

Tires can be changed in less than 10 seconds.

Answer: **True.** When something goes wrong with a car in the middle of a race, the driver pulls into a pit lane. Pit crew mechanics must be able to change tires incredibly quickly.

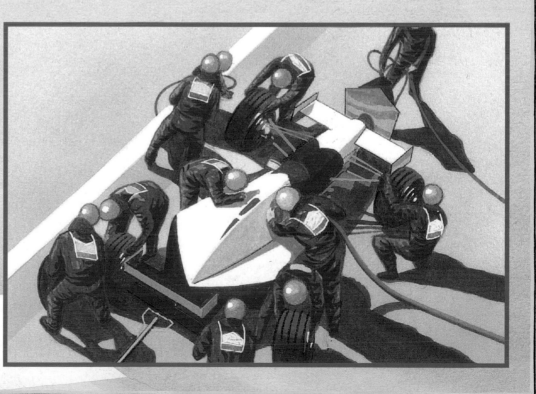

! Driver Juan Fangio won five world championships in seven years.

I didn't know that

some cars need parachutes. Dragsters race 400 meters in less than five seconds! By the end, they are going so fast, they need parachutes to slow them down.

Can you find the oil can?

Rally cars race against the clock over bumpy, off-road courses. The cars have specially strengthened suspension. The driver and the navigator, the person who gives directions, are protected by a steel safety cage.

In the grueling Le Mans 24 Heures, drivers race for a day without stopping. The race used to begin with drivers running to their cars, but this was abandoned because it was too dangerous.

To see how slowly a parachute will fall when it is filled with air, attach a piece of string to each corner of a bandana. Fasten the ends of the strings to a ball of modeling clay. Throw it high into the air.

The longest ever rally is from London to Sydney—19,173 miles (30,857 kilometers)!

I didn't know that

a car can go faster than sound. In October 1997, Thrust SCC became the first car to break the sound barrier. In Black Rock, Nevada, it reached an incredible 766.6 miles (1,233.7 kilometers) per hour!

The 223 mph (360km/h) McLaren F-1 is the fastest road car ever. Underneath, it has fans, which "glue" it to the road.

This odd-looking, pancake-shaped Railton Mobil Special was also a record breaker. Driven by John Cobb in 1947, it reached a speed of 394 mph (634 km/h), exceeding the previous record set by the Thunderbolt by 49 mph (78 km/h).

Donald Campbell broke the land-speed record in 1964, reaching speeds of 431 mph (694 km/h) in his gas-powered Bluebird car.

! In 1994, an electric car traveled at 186 mph (300 km/h).

I didn't know that

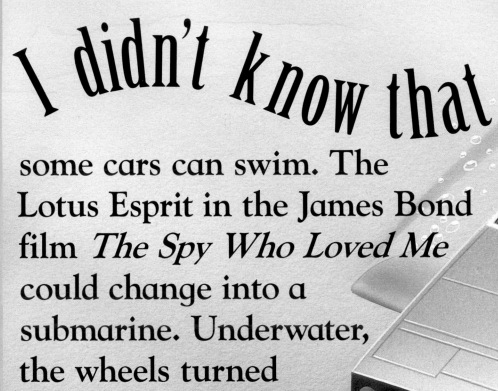

some cars can swim. The Lotus Esprit in the James Bond film *The Spy Who Loved Me* could change into a submarine. Underwater, the wheels turned into propellers.

This funny-looking car is the 1923 Leyat Aerocar. It was pulled along by an enormous wooden propeller at up to 99 mph (160 km/h). However, propellers never became popular.

Can you find the starfish?

116

Cars that regularly drive off the road, like the Range Rover, need to have large, grappling wheels and specially strengthened suspension so they don't get stuck in the mud. They can drive over fields and mountains, across ice, and through rivers.

The Bubble car was briefly popular in the 1950s as a small car for city-dwellers. It had a two-cylinder engine, a door at the front, three wheels, and no reverse gear.

The world's smallest model car is only .026 inches (.67 mm) long.

I didn't know that

some cars have two engines. The Toyota Prius has an electric engine for starting and low speeds, and a gasoline engine, which kicks in when the car reaches a higher speed.

Can you find three rabbits?

This car has been fitted with a solar panel on the roof, which absorbs heat energy from the sun and converts it into electricity. Cars like this need a hot climate. In Australia, there is a race from Darwin to Adelaide, which is exclusively for solar-powered cars.

Some cars are entirely driven by electric motors, not gasoline engines. They are better for the environment, but they can't go very fast and have to be recharged often.

In 1896, some London taxis were electric powered.

I didn't know that

cars in the future will have brains. Cars in the future may be able to think for themselves! They will have a central computer, which will control many of their functions, making them safer and easier to use.

Sensors in the car of the future will be able to detect bumps and potholes in the road ahead, and adjust the suspension accordingly to give the smoothest possible ride.

Using airplane technology, a "head-up display" will project information onto the windshield so that the driver doesn't have to look down at the dashboard. This is much safer, as drivers can concentrate on the road ahead.

On the motorway, computers will be able to measure the distance from the car in front and keep you at a safe distance. You could then drive quickly, but safely.

In the future, cars might drive themselves.

Glossary

Aerodynamic
A shape, like a modern car, which cuts through air easily.

Airbag
A sack which fills with air when a car hits another object. It protects the driver and passengers from injury.

Electric engine
An engine that is powered by electric energy stored in batteries. Electric engines do not produce waste products like those that burn gas or diesel.

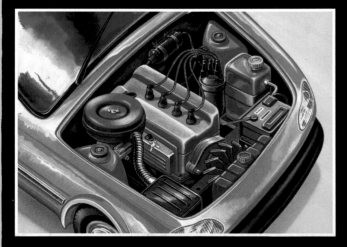

Formula One
The set of rules describing car specifications that Formula One cars have to follow.

Gas engine
An engine that burns gasoline to move a car. Gas engines give off poisonous gases.

Head-up display
The projection of information onto the cockpit of an airplane or the windshield of a car. The drivers can then see it without taking their eyes off where they are going.

Mass-produced
Manufactured on a large scale using machines and people to carry out different parts of the construction process.

Production line
A manufacturing method in which workers are positioned in lines. The work passes from stage to stage.

Solar panel
A device that collects energy from the sun's rays and turns it into electric energy for heating or driving an engine.

Sound barrier
Any vehicle that travels faster than sound waves move through the air (about 1,082 feet, or 330 meters, per second on ground level) is said to have broken the sound barrier.

Suspension
A system of springs or other devices that smooth out the ride of a vehicle.

Road car
A car which is on sale to the public, used for driving on roads instead of in races.

I didn't know that

Concept, editorial, and design by David West Children's Books
Designer: Simon Morse
Illustrators: Ross Watton, Jo Moore
American Edition Editor:Johannah Gilman Paiva
American Redesign: Jonas Fearon Bell

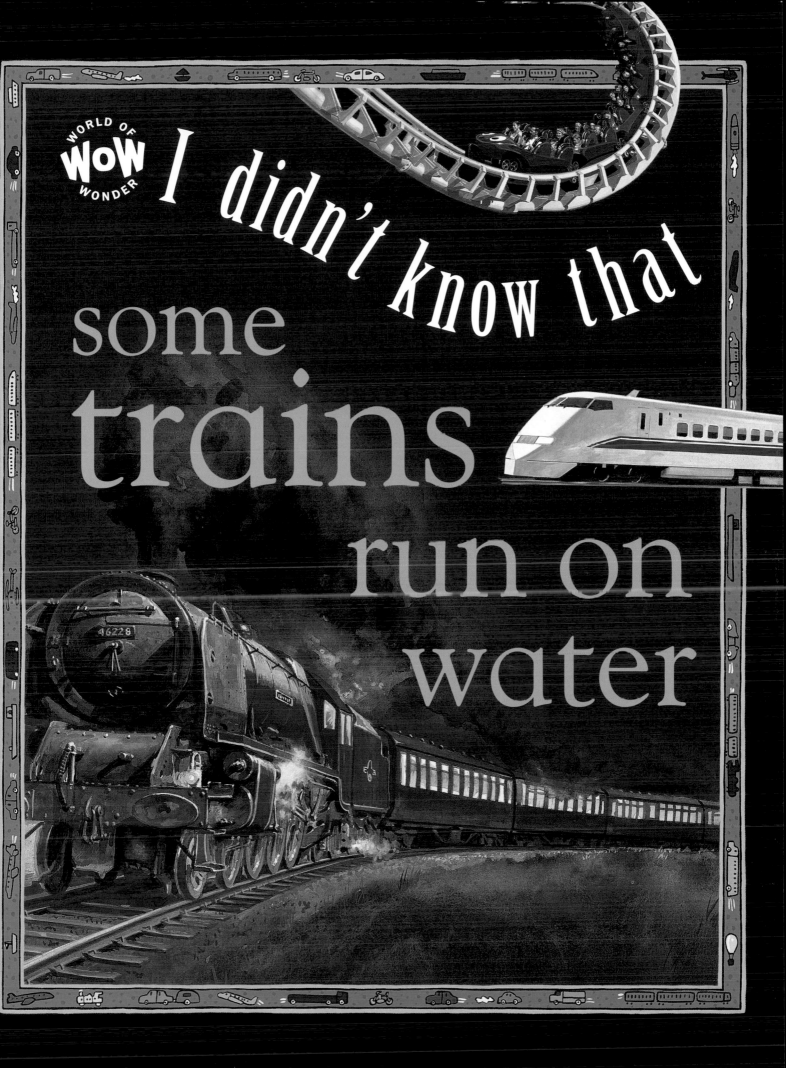

WORLD OF
WOW
WONDER

I didn't know that

some trains run on water

I didn't know that

the first steam trains went slower than walking pace. In 1804, Richard Trevithick's steam engine pulled ten tons of iron ore and 70 passengers over nine miles. It took four hours and five minutes. Trevithick walked ahead all the way.

Can you find the running boy?

In 1829, *Rocket*, built by George Stephenson, won a competition for the best steam engine. It had an average speed of 12 mph and a top speed of 29 mph.

True or False?
Horses pulled the first railroad trains for passengers.

Answer: **True.**
Nearly 200 years ago passengers were pulled by horses on the world's first passenger line in Wales. The Emperor and Empress of Austria used this form of transportation 25 years later (above left).

! *Catch Me Who Can* gave rides to fare-paying passengers.

I didn't know that

steam trains run on water.
A steam engine uses water to get its power.
A coal fire heats the water. The boiling water
turns to steam. The steam is forced into the
cylinders where pistons are pushed that
turn the wheels.

Boiler

Smokestack

Drive wheels

Pistons inside
cylinder

Blast pipes

Hiawatha
steam locomotive

Trains can't always carry enough fuel, so on long journeys they have to stop to take on more fuel and water.

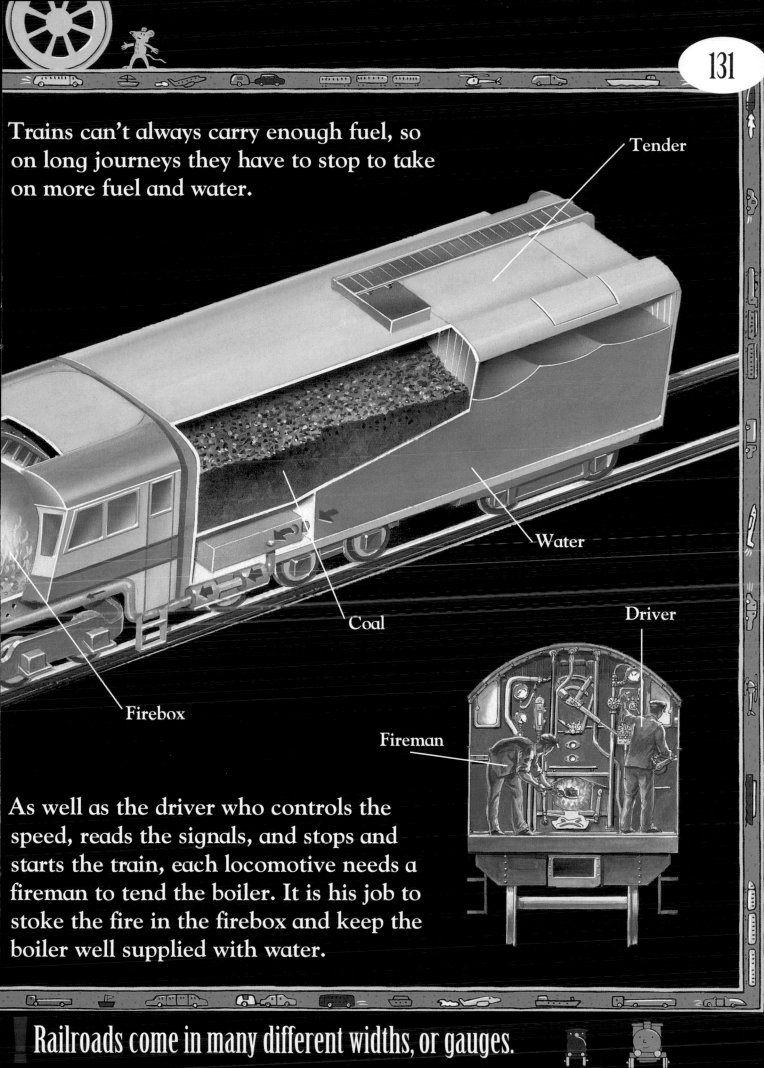

Tender

Water

Coal

Firebox

Driver

Fireman

As well as the driver who controls the speed, reads the signals, and stops and starts the train, each locomotive needs a fireman to tend the boiler. It is his job to stoke the fire in the firebox and keep the boiler well supplied with water.

Railroads come in many different widths, or gauges.

I didn't know that

steam trains opened up the American West. By 1850, the railroad companies had bought the land and laid track from coast to coast. At last goods could get from factories in the East to the new towns in the West.

Can you find the three train robbers?

Two teams built the Union Pacific Railroad across America, starting from opposite ends. They met in Utah in 1869.

True or False?
Casey Jones was a famous train robber.

Answer: **False.**
The real Casey Jones was an engineer who died in 1900 when his engine, the *Cannonball Express*, hit a freight train that was stalled. Casey knew he couldn't slow down fast enough. He made his fireman jump to safety, and all the passengers survived.

Early railroad travelers were often attacked by robbers.

American type 4–4–0 steam locomotive

Before steam trains, settlers traveled in wagon trains.

I didn't know that

the biggest steam locomotive had 24 wheels. *The Big Boy* hauled freight trains on the Union Pacific in the 1940s. This enormous articulated locomotive was nearly 131 feet long.

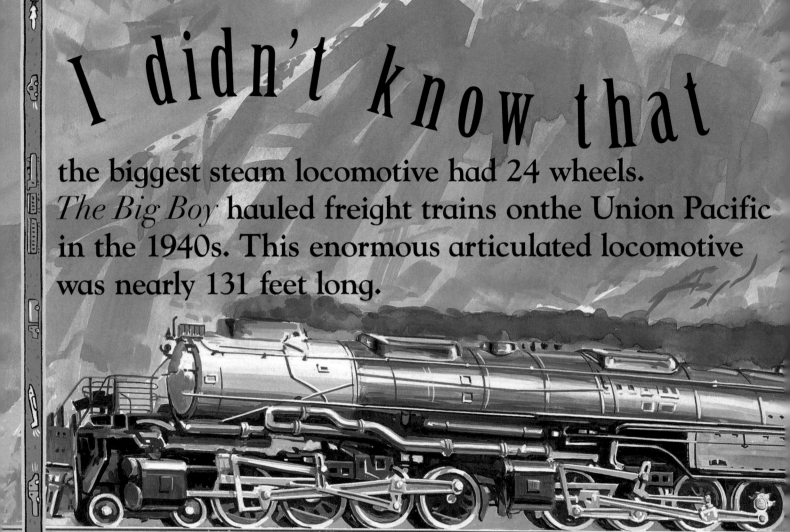

Mallard was a famous streamlined British steam engine. It set the steam speed record of 125 mph in 1938. This record has never been broken!

! One of the longest trains ever pulled 500 cars of coal!

Wheel codes are the numbers used to describe an engine's "wheel combination." The 2-6-2 on the left has 2 leading wheels, 6 driving wheels, and 2 trailing wheels. Can you figure out the wheel codes for A, B, C, and D?

2 - 6 - 2

A

B

C

D

Answers: A. 0-4-0 B. 2-6-0
C. 4-6-4 D. 2-8-2

UNION PACIFIC

4019

This is the 1866 steam locomotive *Peppersass*. It pushed cars up mountains. The wheels and rails were both "toothed" (called "rack and pinion") so they could grip each other.

9

I didn't know that

the *Flying Hamburger* was a train. In 1933, this German diesel-electric two-unit railcar ran at an average speed of 77 miles per hour—proving just how efficient this type of engine could be.

Can
you find
the hamburger?

Most diesel locomotives are in fact diesel-electric, in which the diesel engine makes the electric power to drive the wheels.

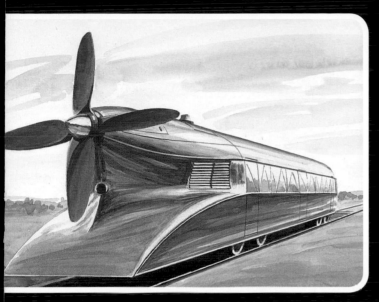

 # True or False? Some trains had propellers.

Answer: **True.**
A diesel engine powered the propeller at the back of the German *Kruckenburg.* It broke the world record in 1931 with an average speed of 143 miles per hour over 6 miles.

Flying Hamburger
two-unit railcar

The *Kitson-Still* of 1924 (right) was diesel driven, but the heat from the diesel engine also heated water to produce steam— for that extra push!

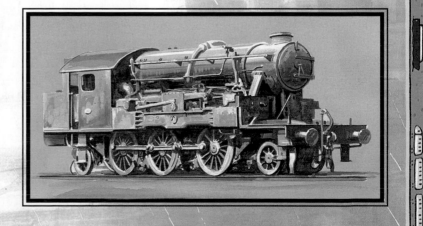

! Diesel trains began to be used in the United States in 1934.

I didn't know that

some trains have several locomotives. Three or four locomotives are often operated by one driver to pull heavy trains. The longest freight train was made up of 16 locomotives and was over several miles long.

Can you find the four Centennials?

6923

UNION PACIFIC

6900 6900

UP 6900

UNION PACIFIC

6900

UNION PACIFIC

Powerful diesel-electric locomotives (below) "shunt" (push or pull) cars over short distances or in freight yards.

The individual cars of a freight train often go to separate destinations. As they pass through the "classification yard," their labels are scanned from the control tower. "Computerized points" then send them in the right direction.

Union Pacific celebrated their 100 years with their new Centennial. 100

I didn't know that

some trains don't make their own power. Some electric trains get their power from overhead wires via a metal pantograph on the roof, others from a conductor rail on the ground.

The *Regio Runners* in Holland (right) are double-decker inter-city trains, powered from overhead electric wires.

French *Class 12000* Electric locomotive

True or False?
There were electric trains more than one hundred years ago.

Answer: **True.**
Werner von Siemens (below) gave a demonstration of his electric locomotive in Berlin in 1879.

Brighton, England.

I didn't know that

trains run beneath the city.
The oldest (1863) and longest
underground system is in London.
Underground rail systems are
now used all over the world.

Thousands of commuters
use Japan's Tokyo
Underground. Attendants
help to shove them onto
the busy trains.

True or False?
Some trains don't need drivers.

Answer: **True.**
The Docklands Light Railway (DLR, right) in London, and the Bay Area Rapid Transit system (BART) that runs under San Francisco Bay are operated from control centers by computers.

A supervisor travels on board the DLR in case anything goes wrong.

Can you find the four mice?

I didn't know that

high-speed trains cruise at 185 mph. The French *TGV* regularly travels at this speed. In 1964, the Japanese *Shinkansen* or Bullet train was the first high-speed train. Now the French *TGV* can equal its top speed.

The high-speed *Shinkansen* takes three hours, and twelve minutes to travel 320 miles from Osaka to Tokyo. How fast is it going?

Shinkansen series 300
High-speed electric Bullet train

Eurostar speeds from London to Paris in three hours. It goes under the English Channel from Folkestone to Calais in only 19 minutes. It is a British design based on the *TGV*.

True or False?
Some high-speed trains lean over when they go around corners.

Answer: **True.**
Trains that lean into curves, like a cyclist on a bicycle, can go faster around bends. Computers on the Italian *ETR* and the Swedish *X2000* (below) tell the train how far to lean as it goes around the bends.

I didn't know that

some trains run on only one rail. A monorail train rides either above or below a single rail. Two vertical wheels guide it along the track and horizontal wheels grip the sides. Sydney's monorail is built on stilts.

The *Ballybunion Line* in Ireland was a monorail system from 1888-1924. Invented by Frenchman Charles Lartigue, the double engine rode on an A-shaped line.

A train with no wheels! *TACV* stands for "tracked air cushion vehicle"– a hovercraft on rails. This experimental Aérotrain is powered by a jet plane's engine.

The power of electromagnets can lift a train above the tracks so that it runs without friction, like this *Maglev* train. If you experiment with two ordinary magnets you will discover just how strong their pulls (attraction) and pushes (repulsion) can be.

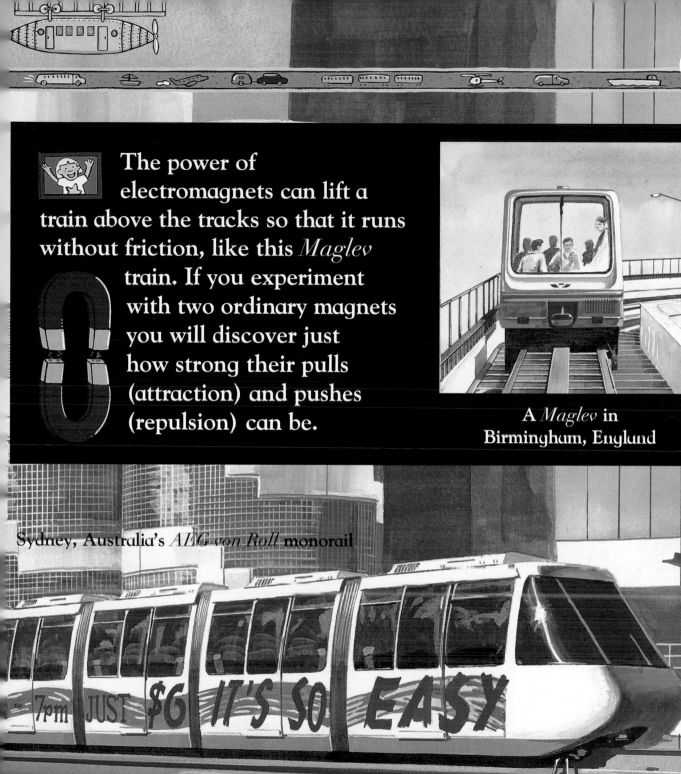

A *Maglev* in Birmingham, England

Sydney, Australia's *AEG von Roll* monorail

I didn't know that

streetcars run on rails in the road. They travel with overhead wires for power. They are popular because they produce less pollution than buses or cars.

Sheffield's Supertram system, England.

Not all trains look like trains. This railcar, built in 1932 for the County Donegal Joint Railways in Ireland, looks much more like a bus!

True or False?
The cars on a cable railroad have electric engines.

Answer: **False.**
The famous cable cars in San Francisco are pulled along by a moving loop of steel cable. The cable runs along a slot in between the rails and the cars clamp onto it.

A diesel railcar in County Donegal, Ireland clocked up nearly one million miles.

I didn't know that

some trains run upside down. Rollercoasters run on rails. They are scary but not dangerous. Speed and gravity secure them. Many have hooks around the rails to hold them safely in place.

Have a whole rail network in your own room! Most models are replicas of full-size trains. They are usually electric.

True or False?
Some miniature trains carry passengers.

Answer: True.
You can visit real miniature railroads and even ride on some of them. This one is steam-powered and is one-fifth the size of the original it has been copied from.

Glossary

Articulated
Built in connected sections. Helps long vehicles go around bends more easily.

Cable railroad
A railroad where passenger cars are pulled along by a moving cable, operated by a stationary motor.

Computerized
Any system that is controlled by computers.

Classification yard
A place where freight cars are shunted (pushed or pulled) to make up trains.

Conductor rail
Electrified rail that passes electricity to an electric train.

Cylinder
Sealed tube in which gas expands to push a piston.

Diesel-electric
On diesel-electric trains the diesel engine powers a generator that provides electricity for the motor.

Gauge
The distance between the two rails on a railroad track.

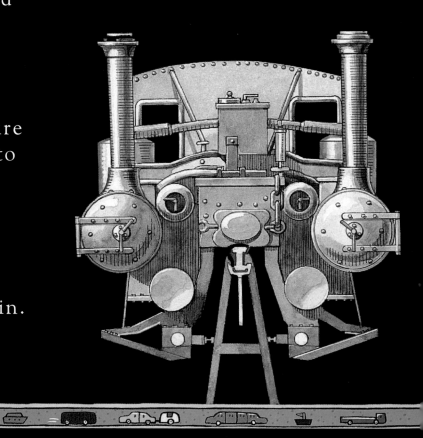

Maglev
Short for "magnetic levitation." A train that is moved along above the track by magnetism.

Monorail
Railcars that run on one rail.

Pantographs
The metal frames on top of an electric train that pick up the electric current from overhead wires.

Piston
The disk that moves inside the cylinder, attached to a rod that turns a crankshaft or flywheel.

Points
A junction where rails can be moved to send a train in a different direction.

Rack and pinion
A system of notched wheels and rails used on mountain railroads.

TACV
Tracked Air Cushion Vehicle—one that moves on a cushion of air above a track.

Wheel combination
The way in which a locomotive's leading (front), driving, and trailing (back) wheels are arranged.

Index